POPE PIUS XII LIBRARY, ST JOSEPH COLLEGE

3 2528 05649 0925

Songs of
KRSNA

D1521307

Songs of
KRSNA

translated by Deben Bhattacharya

SAMUEL WEISER   NEW YORK

ACKNOWLEDGEMENTS

I am deeply indebted to Christopher Nash for generous guidance during my revising the manuscript and for offering many valuable suggestions. I must also express my gratitude to W. G. Archer whose book, *The Loves of Krishna,* London, 1957, has guided me a great deal and particularly with regard to various historical dates.

My thanks are due also to Jharna Bose and Daniel L. Milton for reading the translations and for their constructive suggestions. Finally, I am grateful to Ghanshyam Agrawal who supplied me with the photographs of the Rajasthani miniatures reproduced in this book.

UNESCO COLLECTION OF REPRESENTATIVE WORKS
Indian Series

This book has been accepted in the Indian Literature Translation series of the United Nations Educational, Scientific and Cultural Organization (UNESCO).

English translation, introduction and notes © Copyright UNESCO 1978

ISBN 0-87728-422-9

ISBN 0-87728-421-0 (cloth)
Library of Congress Catalog Card Number: 77-9240

Published in 1978 by
Samuel Weiser, Inc.
740 Broadway
New York, N.Y. 10003

Printed in America
Noble Offset Printers
New York, N.Y.

Contents

Foreword

No other divine or mythical figure in the world has grown in fame as steadily over a period of nearly three thousand years as that of Krishna in India, through the media of religion, poetry and literature, music and painting. Every age in Indian history has contributed to the development of Krishna-lore, and still it continues. Whether Krishna existed historically or not remains a point of controversy in spite of overwhelming proofs in favour of his existence. Nevertheless, his gigantic presence in Indian hearts has made him a symbol of life lived with passion and delight, expressing lyricism and love in the process:

> He was black,
> He had poison eyes.
> A glance from him brought death to my side,
> Life lay open to love's five arrows.[1]

The above description by his beloved herd-girl Radha offers a picture of Krishna but from a particular perspective. This represents a given moment in the wide range of her feelings for him. This is as true a portrait of Krishna as one evoked by her elsewhere, as she views him through another perspective:

---

1. Love Songs of Chandidās, translated by Deben Bhattacharya, London, Allen and Unwin 1967, p. 97; New York, Grove Press, 1970, p. 98.

> I've seen his beauty
> With insatiate eyes.
> His gentle voice
> Brushed my ears.
> Thrilled I long for more. [1]

Krishna has been portrayed with such contrasting colours for over twenty-five centuries. In his looks, he is described as of dark skin, dressed in yellow, and—when young—almost inseparable from his bamboo flute. This he was able to play in such a provocative manner that no girl could resist its call. As he grew older and became involved with the eternal problem of good and evil, the flute was no longer heard. On the contrary, he was seen with his *Pānchajanya,* the conchshell trumpet, calling Arjuna to war against the forces of evil.

Reflecting his various roles Krishna is endowed with an astonishingly long list of names, with each name depicting one of his remarkable deeds, or defining his looks and character. To begin with, Krishna, meaning black, describes the colour of his skin. Pitāmbar means robed in yellow. As the flautist, he is called Banshidhar. His names Govinda and Gopāla, both meaning the cowherd, express his youthful occupation. The name Madhusudan tells us of his slaying the demon Madhu. There are many other names for Kirshna in Sanskrit and in the regional languages of India today. For example, the poetess Mira of Rajasthan frequently uses the name Nandalal (son of Nanda, his foster father) and Giridhāri (for his having lifted the Mount Govardhan in order to protect the cowherds against Indra's wrath). The poet Vidyāpati of Mithila as well as many Bengali poets have often addressed him by his name Mādhava, connected with the season of honey. In Bengali, Shyām (dark, green) Kāliya (suppressor of the serpent Kāliya) and a number of diminutive forms of Krishna, such as Kānu, Kāna, Kānāi, and Kālā are also popular.

---

1. *Love Songs of Vidyāpati,* translated by Deben Bhattacharya and edited by W.G. Archer, London, Allen and Unwin 1963, p. 54. Delhi, Hind Pocket Books, 1967, p. 50; New York, Grove Press, 1970, p. 54.

Radha, too, has been given a number of names but compared to those by which Krishna is known, they are few. In the songs one finds her called Rādhikā, Rāi, Shrimati, and Binodini.

The bulk of the selections in this anthology represents the work of the Bengali poets, including a pair of songs by Jayadeva who wrote in Sanskrit. In addition, a number of Hindi pieces by the great Maithili poet Vidyāpati and by the Rajasthani princess Mirābāi are included.

DEBEN BHATTACHARYA

Note: In the title of this book I have given for the name of Krishna the accepted standard transliteration from Sanskrit. Elsewhere in the book, the more common English spelling is used.

Introduction

The land of Krishna and its folklore

Sprawling along the south bank of the river Jamuna, the thickly populated town of Mathura today is situated at about 125 kilometers southeast of Delhi. As usual in this part of Northern India, the air of Mathura is dry and the climate extreme, the temperature in summer rising to 45° centigrade (113° Fahrenheit) in the shade. The winter is harsh and chilly, although snow does not form on the plains of the Jamuna.

The region of Mathura and its surrounding countryside, including Brindaban (also situated on the banks of the Jamuna), Barsana, Gokul, and Mount Govardhan, is called Braj. The entire pilgrims' route, extending over 84 *krosas*, 280 kilometers (or about 175 miles), is related to Krishna's birth and his life as a youth. The towns and the villages of this area, well connected by roads and footpaths, are dotted with numerous temples, each devoted to a special or a supernatural act of Krishna. Every year, hundreds of thousands of pilgrims from all over India pour into Braj to celebrate the Spring festivals of Barsana and Brindaban in memory of Krishna.

As the pilgrims traverse the springtime landscape, their path in Braj meanders through the domestic scenes of the cowherds' villages, among peasants at work in the fertile plains of the Jamuna where groves of mangoes are radiant with mauve-white blossoms. In Mathura they see the foundations of a temple originally built on the supposed prison ground where Krishna was said to have been born. In a wood at Brindaban, they gaze at trees drooping, as if laden with secrets, and are told that Krishna still visits the wood at night to keep his rendezvous with his beloved herd-girl Radha. In Gokul, too, a whole garden's trees are of a curious sort whose leaves are formed like cups, and the pilgrims are told that Krishna used to drink cream from these leaves. At Govardhan, out of the flat land, there abruptly rises a little hillock that is said to be the Mount Govardhan which Krishna lifted on his little finger to protect the cowherds and the herd-girls from a torrential rain sent down in retaliation by the king of the gods, Indra, who was also the lord of the clouds.[1] Krishna had provoked the cowherds to return to the worship of nature—the forests and the hills which fed them and protected them—rather than Indra. Thus Mount Govardan symbolises a daring act of rebellion against the lord of heaven.

The whole land is full of such concrete mementoes of the legends of Krishna. The rich and living folklore of Braj, spectacular as well as ordinary, its painting, sculpture, architecture, dance, drama, theatre, tales, poetry and songs, continuously remind the trekking pilgrims of the various events of Krishna's life.

In order to plunge the Krishna worshippers into an even deeper awareness of his story, annual folk festivals out of the ancient past re-tell the legend of his birth[2] during the monsoon and, with added intensity, of his romances in the season of delight.

In Spring, the skyline of Braj, shimmering with the approaching summer heat, is festooned with the scarlet blossoms of the flame tree. Perching on leafless branches, these flowers spread out against the blue sky and are called *krishnachurhā*, the crown of Krishna. Bushes of oleander and hybiscus, and the golden acacia sprays fill the woodland where peacocks let out their mating cries and parrots, in millions, add a brighter green to the springtime scene. The entire landscape seems to be preparing for something momentous.

The festival begins. The number of pilgrims multiply overnight as the streets of Mathura, Brindaban, Barsana and the nearby towns and villages are crowded with processions of men, women and

---

1. See plates Nos. 13 and 14.

2. *Janmāstami,* the eighth day following the full moon in the month of August, is celebrated as Krishna's birth anniversary.

children, dancing and singing. Their faces are covered with *ābir*, the red dust, and their clothes are drenched with water colour sprayed from great syringes made of brass. The barriers of caste and class are dropped this day, feuds are set aside and frictions between friends are dispelled by the gaiety of colour. A renewed collective human warmth is introduced into an abstract life of social relationships divided by class and caste. Strangers embrace one another in the streets, smearing the red dust of *ābir* on each other's face.

And in Barsana, which is known as the village of Krishna's principal love, Radha, another kind of drama is re-enacted today amidst cheers, colour and songs. The thick crowd in the narrow village streets line the walls forming a human corridor for the visiting young men from nearby Nandgaon, the village of Krishna. In their hands they carry shields of tortoise-shells. Then, all of a sudden, from the opposite direction enter the girls of Barsana, all modestly dressed in *sāris* and veils but armed with long bamboo sticks. The men raise their shields to defend themselves as the girls set upon them. The music goes silent. Only the random beating of the sticks against the hard tortoise-shells is heard, and occasional voices from the crowd crying out for mercy. But the girls of Radha's village are bent upon avenging Krishna's misbehaviour toward Radha. They drop their sticks only after chasing the boys away.

Love and violence, laughter and colour, food and drink, songs and dances, are all inseparably interwoven through the day of the full moon of Spring.[1]

From the folk traditions of Braj we learn several important facts about Krishna's early life:

Born in the prison of Kansa, the tyrant king of Mathura, Krishna was smuggled out by his father, Vasudeva; for Kansa had decided to destroy the child. At the suggestion of his mother Devaki, Krishna was taken to Gokul, to the house of Nanda and Yashoda.

---

1. *Dol Purnima* or *Holi,* the day of the Spring festival, falls usually in February or March, depending on the date of the first full moon in Spring.

Although he was brought up as a modest cowherd, Krishna was endowed with the unusual capacity to destroy a great number of evil spirits and to defy even Indra, the Vedic ruler of heaven. His final act in this part of India was to kill Kansa and supervise the rule of Mathura until order was restored.

The simple cowherds of Braj, though immensely impressed by his superhuman powers, treated him as one of them, like a brother, without the distance or awe due to a divine being.

And above all, Krishna, the cowherd of Braj, ruled supreme not only as the lord of Radha and the master of the hearts of the herd-girls, but as the imperial sovereign over the human, animal and vegetable worlds. His flute enchanted all. Its sound echoed in the ears of the cowherds and the herd-girls of Gokul and Brindaban alike, even when Krishna had left them to launch himself in his career as a political leader and a strategist.

With his army of the Yādavas, he moved to Dwarka, on the western seacoast, never to return to Braj.

Krishna of the Sanskrit literature

Krishna does not appear in the earliest surviving literature of the Sanskrit language, the Vedas, whose date of origin is variously estimated to have been in the period between 3000 BC and 1500 BC. The Vedic gods, in the main, represent the elemental forces, such as Indra, Varuna (water), Agni (fire), Surya (the sun) and others. Krishna was either unknown to the authors of the Vedas or he was considered too unconventional for the galaxy of the Vedic gods.

Following the Vedic period, an important new literature called the Upanishads began to accumulate over several centuries. The Upanishads, based on dialogues between masters and disciples, enquired into the nature of life and death, the concept of re-incarnation, and finally, man's relationship to God.

The *Jivātmā*, which is often translated as 'soul' or 'self', is the basis of being. Like God, it has no birth nor death. It has no physical attributes. The *Jivātmā* pervades the entire being of man including his flesh, feelings and thoughts, and yet remains wholly free. Man's ultimate achievement rests in the realisation that the *Jivātmā* is indivisible and, therefore, inseparable from God, the *Paramātmā*. Until this realisation has taken place through conscious discipline and deeds, the life of man moves from existence to existence, in a recurring cycle of birth and death. Life, in this context, can be compared to a potter's workshop where each piece of pottery is part of the greater space. Its shape and size are determined by the conscious act of the potter. The concept of re-incarnation can be described as an aid to man's freedom from his primitive fear of death.

It is in one of these recorded dialogues, called the *Chhāndogya Upanishad*, we meet Krishna for the first time as an inconspicuous student listening to his master, the sage Ghora, as the latter discourses on the theory of re-incarnation. The fact that Krishna—who is described in the later literature as a re-incarnation of Vishnu, the preserving god of the Hindu Triple-forces[1]—should be presented in this off-hand manner, suggests that the compilers of the Upanishad were unfamiliar with his actual role in folklore and in the epic. Considered to have been compiled during the sixth century BC[2], the *Chhāndogya Upanishad* can be described as a posthumous record of Krishna's dialogue with the sage.

The Buddha was born during the fifth century BC and in the general enthusiasm over Buddhism in Northern India, Krishna is rarely referred to in the extant Sanskrit literature of the next few centuries. This sluggish pace continued until approximately 400 AD, when the kaleidoscopically detailed epic, the *Mahābhārata*, begun some eight centuries before, had assumed the coherent form which we now associate with it.

The modest scholar of metaphysics, the Krishna of the *Chhāndogya Upanishad*, emerges with terrifying self-assurance and splendour in the second act of his appearance in Sanskrit literature. In the *Mahābhārata*, the reader is led to realize that the authors of the epic were well acquainted with the nature of Krishna in his youth as portrayed by the folklore of Braj. In the epic, however, he is

---

1. The other two being Brahma, the creator, and Shiva, the destroyer.

2. W.G. Archer in *The Loves of Krishna,* 17.

presented differently—as a full-blooded adult, more matured and sophisticated and possessed of a controlled sensuality. Here he is given the role of leading the war at Kurukshetra which is viewed as having taken place circa 1400-1000 BC [1].

As two related families, the Pāndavas and the Kauravas, extended their private feud into a bloody war, Krishna gave a choice to the rival parties and following their decision, he presented himself as a consultant to the Pāndavas and his formidable army of the Yādavas to their enemy. As charioteer of Arjuna, one of the Pāndava brothers, Krishna led the eighteen days' war to its victorious end but at an incalculable cost. Together with innumerable heroes on both sides, both the Kauravas and the sons of the Pāndavas were wiped out. Only the five Pāndava brothers were left alive at the end of this epic war. In winning it, Krishna had used every device within his power. Whenever at a fatal turning point on the battlefield of Kurukshetra, treachery was Krishna's order of the day. The rogue of Braj, who had broken many a heart by his enchanting deceits, had developed his amoral talents into military cunning.

Arjuna challenged him many times and came to the point of complete psychological collapse upon seeing friends and kinsmen slaughtered by the thousands. But Krishna would not budge until the evil Kauravas were vanquished. Here too, we find the folklore of Braj echoing this death of evil on an epic scale.

In the brilliant war reportage of the *Bhagavad Gitā,* of possibly the second century BC [2], Krishna offers some explanations of his unsoldierly counsels on the battlefield. But these can be accepted only as a sermon from the mouth of Vishnu incarnate. In a battle between good and evil, the evil must lose whatever the cost.

Although there is a feeling of continuity in the development of Krishna's character from his folkloric youth to his epic maturity, the *Mahābhārata* does not dwell upon the stories of Krishna's early life in

1. M.A. Mehendale, *The Age of Imperial Unity.* 251, quoted by W.G. Archer in *The Loves of Krishna,* 115.

2. W.G. Archer, *The Loves of Krishna,* 115.

Braj which belonged to his past and private life and thus was no part of the main theme of the epic. According to the Indian social custom this was and is good taste.

For the first time in Sanskrit literature, the *Bhāgavat Purāna* of the ninth or tenth century AD[1] takes some serious notice of the folklore of Braj. The *Purāna* follows his biographical pattern, stage by stage, starting from his birth in the dungeon of Kansa in Mathura; it tells of his childhood as a cowherd in Gokul, his romances with the herd-girls, the annihilation of the evil spirits including Kansa, and finally, of the events leading up to his departure for Dwarka as a prince, accompanied by the Yādavas. But the *Bhāgavat Purāna*, too, like the *Mahābhārata*, discreetly avoids any mention of Radha, Krishna's principal beloved among the adoring herd-girls.

Following the tales of the initial period at Braj, the *Purāna* further steadily unfolds the episodes of Krishna's life, sequence after sequence, through his first marriage to the princess Rukmini and his succeeding ones to seven other queens, his roles in war and peace, and his status as a divine incarnate. The *Purāna* also deals with his additional sixteen thousand and one hundred wives and their children.

But time is relentless. Krishna's corporeal being is destined to dissolve in the process of his final union with Vishnu. His formidable army of the Yādavas, without his personal control, show themselves to be as capable of evil and destruction in the lives of the righteous as are the demons whom he has suppressed. A train of events is set in motion. The Yādavas take to drinking and engage in a suicidal fist fight.

In the final scene, Krishna, the hero of such a fantastic drama, having lived the entire compass of life envisioned on a superrealistic scale, dies bleeding under a fig tree. While he sleeps, an unknown hunter mistakes his foot for a gazelle's ear and charges his arrow. The forest worshipper of Braj is killed by a forest dweller. But with no malice.

---

1. W.G. Archer, *The Loves of Krishna*, 25.

Krishna and the arts

Following the circulation of the *Bhāgavat Purāna* and the slow dissipation of Buddhism from the Indian scene, the theme of Krishna found a renewed life through religion and the arts. From the eleventh century onwards, the Vaishnava[1] religious movements developed on a wide scale, and eventually reached most parts of India: Rāmānu-jāchārya (AD 1037-1137), Mādhvāchārya (AD 1199-1303) and Nimbārka in Southern India; Vallabhāchārya (born 1479) and Shri Chaitanya (AD 1486-1533) in Northern India are considered among the most revered leaders of the Vaishnava faith.

The path of *bhakti,* or the belief in the mystical love for or devotion to a personalised god, is the essence of this popular religious movement. In its view, since there is no separation between the creator and the created, a man has no reason to focus his mind only on the abstract concept of God who has no shape, sex or attributes. He may therefore choose his own favorite statue of Krishna, install it at home or in a temple, and if he can place his complete faith and devotion in this ephemeral symbol of the eternal being, he may achieve union with God.

As with most Hindu sects, of which Vaishnavism is an important example, this religious movement is not dependent on a prophet but is fulfilled by collective thinking and collective effort. The contributions of artists, in this respect, have been invaluable in spreading the Vaishnava faith of devotion and love.

Radha, who seems to have been so deliberately neglected by the authors of the epic and so cautiously avoided by the biographers of the *Bhāgavat Purāna,* now suddenly appears like a queen in the full majesty of love. The twelfth century Bengali poet, Jayadeva, of the *Gita Govinda*—Songs of the Cowherd—opens his collection of songs in Sanskrit by saying:

---

1. Vaishnava means 'related to Vishnu'. Because Krishna is Vishnu incarnate, the Krishna worshippers are known as Vaishnavas. Similarly, the arts and letters connected with Krishna are called Vaishnava arts or Vaishnava literature.

Clouds soften the sky
and the *tamālas* cast their shadow on the forest floor.
Krishna is afraid of his act last night,
Radha, guide him home.
At Nanda's direction the lovers walked
toward the grove that shored the river
in a glory of secret love[1].

Because the *Gita Govinda* was written in Sanskrit, it was comprehensible to many in all parts of India. The theme of the *Gita Govinda,* dealing with Radha and Krishna's love in different stages of its development, including that in which the painful uncertainty on Radha's part as to Krishna's fickleness leads finally to their passionate union, made its impact on all branches of the arts.

Jayadeva's songs, meant to be sung in the classical modes of the Indian Raga system, served as the model for later poets. Each song was given a Raga, a melodic form belonging to a particular scale. Following Jayadeva, the thirteenth century poet Bilvamangala of Kerala and the poets of the fifteenth century and after—namely, Vidyāpati[2] of Mithila, Chandidās[3] of Bengal, Mirābāi of Rajasthan, Surdās from the Hindi speaking regions of Northern India and many others—wrote an astonishing number of songs on Radha and Krishna's love in practically all the regional languages of India.

Owing to the influence of Shri Chaitanya, the fifteenth-century Bengali leader of the Vaishnava faith, further interesting developments occurred in Bengal. New styles in the presentation of songs in praise of Krishna, accompanied by a special barrel-shaped drum called

---

1. This opening verse has been interpreted variously by different scholars. One interpretation suggests that Krishna's foster father Nanda had asked Radha to escort Krishna, then a small boy and frightened of the approaching night, to his home, and that on their way they had made love in the forest grove.

2. See *Love Songs of Vidyāpati,* translated by Deben Bhattacharya and edited by W.G. Archer; London, 1963.

3. See *Love Songs of Chandidas,* translated by Deben Bhattacharya, London, 1967.

the *khol* and a small pair of bell metal cymbals, were introduced. The story of Radha's estrangement from Krishna after his adventures with other herd-girls, of Krishna's appeasement of Radha, and finally, of the reunion of the lovers, is the subject of these songs, presented with spoken commentaries by the leading singers. As a result of the widespread popularity of the themes, a new school of lyric poetry, now called the Vaishnava songs, grew up during the centuries that followed Chandidās, the fifteenth century Bengali poet. More than two hundred poets have been acclaimed as authors of such works, writing over a period of close to four hundred years.

Over the centuries, classical schools of dance-drama such as Bharatanātyam and Kathakali in the south, Manipuri in the north-east, and the courtly Kathak of the north and north-west, adopted the Krishna theme as an important motif for dramatic expression. Independent of the classical schools, the folk theatre of Braj (called the Krishnalilā, the Krishna play) and that of Bengal (called the Jātrā) began to draw even larger audiences to the dramatic presentation of the legends of Krishna. As a matter of fact, the courtly presentation of the Kathak dance can be described as a development of the folkloric Krishnalilā.

In the realm of sculpture, some of the oldest works showing Krishna as Vishnu's incarnation appear as early as the seventh century, in the rock-cut temples at Mamallapuram, on the south-east coast. Themes from the folklore of Braj, connecting Krishna with the cowherds and herd-girls, the lifting of the Mount Govardhan, and certain episodes from the epic *Mahābhārata,* are marvelously wrought in stone in this temple. Here, in addition, is further evidence that the legends of Braj had already been circulating in different parts of India even before the authors of the *Bhāgavata Purāna* began to record the biography of Krishna.

Sculpture, as a more popular craft, has also continuously employed the Krishna themes, but we have no means of assessing the date of its commencement. Even today, the images of Radha and Krishna's youth and his principal love, Radha. The elaborately detailed bronze, stone, wood and clay, provide a living for a large number of traditional craftsmen all over India. Those in bronze, stone and wood are designed to be installed in temples or in family shrines. The clay images, on the other hand, are for worship at annual occasions such as the Spring festival or the celebration of the birthday of Krishna. Once the ceremony is over, the clay figures are immersed in the river according to the Indian tradition of symbol worship.[1]

As to the field of painting, although Western India produced one of the earliest available illustrated versions of the *Gita Govinda* in or about 1450 AD, the theme of Radha and Krishna's romance was not taken up as a popular subject until the 17th century. Once the divine romance was accepted as subject matter for the art of miniature painting, different schools under princely patronage between the seventeenth and the nineteenth centuries produced a large collection of the most exquisitely lyrical illustrations. A number of them came from Rajasthan and others represented various regional styles including the renowned schools of the Punjab Hills.

Krishna and the contemporary world

The folklore of Braj does not provide us with any clue as to the dates of origin of the tales, customs or place-names connected with Krishna's youth and his principle love, Radha. The elaborately detailed folklore of Braj involving the names of cities and villages, hills and rivers connected with Krishna must have taken many centuries of oral tradition to develop—possibly prior to the emergence of the Sanskrit literature about him.

Krishna has remained astonishingly popular for over 2000 years in Indian arts and literature and possibly much longer in folklore. This may be attributed in part to his association with Vishnu. However, long before Krishna, there had already been seven incarnations of Vishnu[2], including the prince Rama of Ayodhya who,

---

1. While the worship of the idol is to assist man in his spiritual development, an essential aspect of this development is the disciple's rejection of personal attachment to the physical object, the idol itself.

2. Mina (fish), Kurma (tortoise), Varāha (boar), Narasimha (man-lion), Vāmana (the dwarf) and Parashurāma (Rama carrying an axe) who had exterminated the Kshatriyas, the martial caste, twenty-one times; and Rama, prime of Ayodhyā, hero of the Ramayana.

too, has inspired the arts and has been honoured by an equally great epic, the *Rāmāyana*. Following Krishna, the Buddha of the fifth century BC is considered a further incarnation of Vishnu. But none of these has presented such baffling contradictions nor inspired so vast a wealth of art objects as Krishna.

Although both Rama and the Buddha have been equally honoured before and after Krishna, their lives, while exceptional, have followed patterns which are close to accepted norms: they have consistently remained righteous and idealistic.

Krishna, on the other hand, has trifled with social ethics just as readily as he has vigorously defended the members of society against all evil. As a boy, he took delight in stealing milk and cream, and lied unscrupulously. While his foster mother, Yashoda, occasionally punished him for it, the women of Braj doted over this precocious child who was equally capable of killing fearful demons. We see the same characteristics persist as Krishna, the enchanting youth, develops into a gallant libertine. Girls of Braj—from beautiful Radha to Kubja the hunchback of Mathura—tumble before his wayward charm. Although he returns again and again to Radha, he manages to keep his mistresses eternally captivated by the careful distribution of his affection and of his deceits. When in a critical predicament, he is always prepared to escape by the grace of his private arsenal of supernatural powers. Once, on a night of the full moon, when the herd-girls of Braj had gathered in the forest, all passionately eager to dance alone with Krishna, he was forced to produce multiple replicas of himself.[1] Each maiden to dance with Krishna had dissolved in delight, alas, only to discover that the rogue had fled together with his other, favourite girl.

In the next stage of development, we find Krishna installed as a prince in Dwarka. Far away from Braj, both in time and space, he is no longer the frivolous youth but a mature man. And yet, the basic pattern of his character remains constant even though the events are different. He is first married to the princess Rukmini but his interest in life remains as intense as ever. Although he is no longer the fickle

---

1. See illustrations Nos. 18 and 19.

romancer of Braj, he has been married to seven other women and then, as we are told by the *Bhāgavata Purāna,* to a crowd of sixteen thousand and one hundred girls, all of whom, we are further told, bore him children.

Most of all, while he raced through life with stupendous avidity for love and women, besides destroying demons and evil spirits for righteous causes, he was constantly being called upon for help whenever human dignity was threatened.

Before the Kurukshetra war, when Duryodhan, the elder Kaurava brother, begins publicly to strip Draupadi, the joint wife of the five Pāndava brothers, Krishna intervenes though he remains unseen. As Duryodhan pulls and gathers one end of the *sāri* of a confused Draupadi, Krishna maintains an undetected but endless supply at the other end. Exhausted and shamed, Duryodhan finally gives up in this attempt of his to humiliate the Pāndavas.

And as the two rival families decide to engage in a war, Krishna is immediately there, trying to mediate for a peaceful settlement. But the forces of evil have the upper hand and refuse peace. Krishna persists in being just; he offers his mighty army of the Yādavas to one family and himself unarmed, to the other, leaving the decision of choice to the warring families. The Kauravas decide for the Yādavas and the Pāndavas for Krishna. Once the decision is reached and the war declared, Krishna plunges headlong into it.

The Kauravas have managed to muster practically all the great warriors of the period to their side. The Pāndavas, on the other hand, have hardly anything to fight with apart from their own courage and the wit and the brilliance of Krishna, who, in any case, will not fire a weapon. Always in the frontline, as he drives Arjuna's chariot, Krishna constantly cajoles and nags Arjuna and other Pāndava warriors to adopt unethical military measures so that the ultimate victory of the righteous party is assured. The enchanting deceptions of Braj have developed into a frightening political and moral strategy. The greatest preacher of action for action's sake, independent of the concern for results[1], is now wholly committed to the war at

---

1. *Bhagavad Gita,* III.

Kurukshetra. Eighteen infernal days ensue. The great Bhisma of the Kaurava side, who is also equally loved and respected by the Pāndavas, succumbs in a fatal charge. To the Pāndavas the fall of such a hero upon the battle-scarred earth is an unbearable indignity. They collect their forces with lightning speed and fire thousands of rounds to provide a cushion of arrowheads for the falling hero even though he has belonged to the enemy camp. Human dignity and the respect for life's unavoidable realism are the underlying spirit of the Kurukshetra war.

Krishna, the object of women's passions and of great men's adoration, dies as modestly and naturally as a grass flower, when an unknown hunter shoots him[1] by mistake. Krishna lived his life fully but his death was a simple, routine affair. This lack of drama at the end of a life which is so full of dramatic events, is consistent with Krishna's character and his sense of human dignity even though his final destination is heaven and union with Vishnu.

The reason for Krishna's continuous appeal for so many centuries seems to depend on various factors. His deep engagement with the basic elements of nature—hills and rivers, trees and animals, men and women, war and peace, good and evil—has enriched his character to such an extent that the role of Krishna, including the contradictions, represents the very nature of life itself. While the other incarnations of Vishnu, such as Prince Rama and the Buddha, preached idealism of a puritanic type, Krishna—without being materialistic—sponsored men's faith in the reality of life.

---

1. A.L. Basham in *The Wonder that was India,* 305, suggests that the circumstances of Krishna's death are 'quite un-Indian in their tragic character'. Mr. Basham further declares that such situations are 'well known in European epic literature, but do not occur elsewhere in that of India'. The scenes toward the close of the epic *Ramayana* when Sita, humiliated and hurt, disappears into the earth in front of a confused and lamenting Rama are in fact more tragic than the scenes related to Krishna's death and are comparable with many of those moments in European epic literature to which Basham would refer. In fact there is no shortage of tragic situations in either the epic literature or the drama of India; rather, they are simply treated differently from those of their European counterparts. Tragedy is merely one of the basic moods of the Indian dramatic arts whereas it marks the climax in European tradition. Krishna's death does not bring the epic *Mahabharata* to its conclusion nor do the Indians treat the *Bhagavata Purāna* as a record of dramatic tragedy.

By challenging the power of Indra, the lord of heaven, in favour of the cowherds' worship of the landscape and the growing things of this earth, Krishna tried a marriage of faiths, a wedding of the nature spirits of tribal India with the elemental gods of the Vedic Aryans whose abode was heaven. In seeking a unity between these two worlds, Krishna had succeeded in delighting both. As a result, in spite of his return to Vishnu's heaven, he appears to be eternally alive on the earth but transmuted to a scale that is spanned by nothing less than the full breadth and stature of the arts and letters concerning him which India has continued to produce for more than twenty centuries.

Songs of KRSNA

Jayadeva

❖❖❖❖❖❖❖❖❖❖❖❖❖❖❖❖❖❖❖❖❖❖❖❖❖❖❖❖❖

Raga Vasanta [1]
The southern breeze
is softened by the enchanting
clove-scented vines
and the woodland hut is tuned
by the blended song of the humming honey-bees
and the cooing of the *kokilas.* [2]
The parted ache, dear friend,
while in this delicious Spring
Krishna   dances with the youthful girls— [3]
sporting, loving.

Maddened by passion,
as girls with straying loves
lament their loss,
bees, in waves, descend
on the flowers of Spring.

Buds on the branches of the *tamāla* trees
rule the air with their musk.
The blossoming claws of the scarlet *palāsha*
—fierce as the nails of the God of love—
tear the heart of the young apart.
While the petals of *pātali,*
prickled by bees,
appear as the quiver of Love's five arrows,
the golden *keshar,* the sceptre of desire,
is lord of the land.

Flowering cirtus laughs at the world—
Shameless in Spring.
Laughter, laughter, in all directions
as those with pain of parting fall,

pierced by the spearlike *ketaki*,
the open teeth of the fragrant grass.

Vibrant with the perfume of sweet flowers,
the season of Spring, a friend of the young,
lures the ascetic astray.
As stalwart trees tremble with delight
clasped in desire by blossom-laden vines,
the Jamuna washes the shores of Brindāban
and in forests flourishes the Spring.

---

1. See illustration Nos. 20 and 21.
2. *Kokila*, the Indian Cuckoo. Its cry is said to represent the perfect
   fifth of the Indian octave. The bird is associated with Spring-time
   and love.
3. In the original poem, Krishna is addressed here by his name Hari,
   the remover of pain.

Raga Gurjari
Seeing me besieged
by a bouquet of beauties from the cowherd clan,
Radha has walked away.
Aware of my wayward ways, I panicked
and failed to stay her.
God, O God,
she left unadored,
in anger, and in injured pride.

While parting presses so endlessly long—
how does she behave?
And what does she say?
And here I am in a world of gaiety and wealth,
of friends and a home,
useless, sundered from her.

I recall her face
flushed with the weight of anger
and her eye-brows curled quivering
like anxious bees over a scarlet lotus bloom.
I feel her presence in my heart
and mine in hers, in a union of love.
Why then do I seek her in the wilderness,
moaning, meaninglessly?

Your heart, I understand, my slender girl,
is tortured by jealousy.
I do not know where you are gone
and I cannot pray to appease you.
And yet, in my vision you seem to stir,
going, coming, before my eyes
while in vain I long for your loving arms,
as in the olden days.

Never again shall I behave this way.
Have forgiveness, I beg of you.
My beautiful love,
pained by my passionate will,
I beseech you to come forth.

Vidyāpati

❖❖❖❖❖❖❖❖❖❖❖❖❖❖❖❖❖❖❖❖❖❖❖❖❖

I wish water would wash away
this my day of shame.

As I climbed the steps
to the Jamuna bank,
my skin was glistening
through my thin, wet clothes
and all my limbs
were open to view
when Krishna descended upon me.
I tried to cover
the curves of my thighs
with my hair by cowering down.
He fixed his gaze upon my breasts
but I turned my back on him.
And Krishna, unyielding, smiled at me
as I helplessly struggled
to hide myself.

Vidyāpati retorts: You silly girl,
Why didn't you rush to the river again.

O friend,
My love has left for that terrible land:
where *kokilas* do not sing,
bees do not hum
and flowers do not blossom in the wood.
Where the seasons do not change,
and love has no power.
Where the people do not speak
nor hear of love.
And my love has marched to that fearful land . . .

My heart is filled with shame—
have I only been a fool?
Has Krishna then no taste
for the art of loving?

In that night of rains
as I walked to your doors,
snakes hissed at my feet
and the darkness grew deep.

Listening to the sound of desire
as I stood stabbed
by love's five arrows,
my heart shrank at my daring.
Am I rejected then,
my man of miracles?

I shall close down the tryst
for all women.
That sport of love,
this wonder of passion,
is only a faraway cry.
Even beholding you
fills me with doubts.

The night is crawling to the fourth watch,
I must now go home . . .

The night vomits lamp-black.
As fierce snakes straggle
on the path to the tryst,
lightning crashes with fearful force
and clouds in wrath explode.

Dear love, I shy of shaping words.
And yet, with courage in my heart today,
I resigned myself to my fate.
Shall we then fulfill our promise
and let it befall us?
Heart knows no limits.

~~~~~~~~~~~~~~~~~~~~~~~~~~~~~~~~~~~~~~~

My eyes pursued his path
till they were swollen.
And yet Krishna never came.

I can no longer bear my life.
My hopes have withered away, my lord.
I wish to fly to that land
where Krishna could be found
and love's philosopher's stone
would change my heart to a heart of gold . . .

The wretched sea
that houses the wicked moon
may burn to ashes.

Love has no lyrics for it now!
As a girl, drowning in disgrace,
longs for her lover's return,
time slowly dies
over a liar's guaranty . . .

Krishna has forgotten
the hour of the tryst.

Dear friend,
the night was a pack of tales!
A precious stone fell in his hands
but the fool of a jeweller
could not tell
gold from a piece of glass.
He valued as equal
jewels and the gem-weigher's beads.
He never learned the arts of love,
milk and water
were one and the same.
How could I share delicious joys
with such as him? . . .

Hard as thunder
is your heart
but your words flow
as life-bestowing nectar.
I did not know
how cunning you were.
My thoughts and hopes
were far from yours.
I saw myself
slide down the evil path
with crippled dignity.
I regret not thinking
before I acted.
But how can you show your face
from the depth of a well,
hidden with leaves?
You did not honour your words . . .

When the storm exploded
and the rain came,
I took shelter under a tree
dreaming to save my life.
The tree crashed down
upon my head.
The sea of love
ran shallow on me.
I am burdened with blame.

Go, then, Mādhava, go.
I have nothing more to say.
My doomed words fall
like splinters of stone.
Turning silent as I speak,
the castaway stones are received by the earth.

My sadness has no end, dear friend.
Weighed down with clouds
this month of rains,
my home is hollow and void.
Clouds accumulate
forever roaring
and how the rain falls
all over the world.
My lord holidays
while I ache in love.
Clouds pierce me with arrows,
the peacocks dance in joy,
the drunken frogs
make merry in the fields
but the cries of the monsoon birds
burst open my heart.
Darkness engulfs the night
restless with lightning
that flashes
line upon line.

I was unaware
of the power of love
and I thought my lover
was forever mine.
Bewitched,
I had taken shelter in his love
but to be bitterly dispossessed.

While I prayed
and offered my life,
my love abruptly departed
without a single word.
I hold his loveliness now
in the core of my heart
but as a constant pain.
And I live only for the moment,
like a lamp without oil.

~~~~~~~~~~~~~~~~~~~~~~~~~~~~~~~~~~~~~

Mādhava has gone away
to the city of Mathura.
The jewel that shone
over the village Gokula
is stolen away forever.
Gokula flooded with torrents of tears,
is awash with cries of pain.
The village is eroded of life.
And my home gapes at me
with the emptiness
of the entire horizon . . .

Friend, at its softest spot
my heart, like a doe,
is struck
by the hunter's arrow.
Oh why did I give him
that half-glance! . . .
I heard his heart-enticing flute,
my doubts dissolved.
The banks of the river,
the forest of *kadamba* trees
and the steps to the water
grew near.
I turned back
to see if he was coming:
I stumbled and my feet
were ravaged by thorns.

Torrents of tears flow from her eyes.
Who can watch the monsoon break?
The moon climbs the mountain peaks
in terror of eclipse . . .
Her brooding face
is lolling on her breasts.
O friend,
how can I describe her state?

The wind vomits fire,
the sandal breeze poison.
Cold resolves into heat.
The moon is hotter than the sun.
Can life continue?
Moon, sun and sandal breeze
combine to burn her.
Stricken by the arrows of love
She can never be cured.
Though she drinks
immortal nectar,
she cannot live without you.

Chandidās
❖❖❖❖❖❖❖❖❖❖❖❖❖❖❖❖❖❖❖❖❖❖❖❖❖

Yes, my lord of delight,
you do well
in wrecking the honour of love.
But frets have
reduced me to nought,
and I am known
only to the world by my disgrace . . .

~~~~~~~~~~~~~~~~~~~~~~~~~~~~~~

Day and night
as I wonder and brood,
my sorrows grow.
If I had wings
I would fly away
and never show my face again.
O friend,
Krishna has hurt me . . .

The ignorant shout at me
saying, "Out, out with you,
you scandalous slut!"
And I cannot divine
whom I have robbed.
None ever speak to me
and I live in ceaseless fear.
But this is a disgraceful lie
since he and I are not on speaking terms . . .

~~~~~~~~~~~~~~~~~~~~~~~~~~~~~~

. . . I met a connoisseur
of the flavours of love,
and desire mounted in me.
O my life's dear love,
as I counted the nights for you,
flames of fire rose in my heart,
spreading and growing,
till I was bodily scorched by love . . .

Friend, do not take his name.
Love of the black one is an agony
that haunts life long.

My eyes reject the dark river[1]
and the word black is mute to my tongue.
And yet, Kālā, the black one,
keeps vigil in my heart—
and his name I repeat
as a prayer, with my beads.

I shall say goodbye to all
and leave this world
to lose myself in the deep forest.

———————

1. Kālindi, Jamunā.

I am a prisoner of your love,
my lord of delight—
my heart, wholly with you,
can feel nothing else.
Awake or in dream,
lost in my thoughts,
I behold your beautiful face
and I etch it on the earth.

Sitting with the elders,
if I ever hear your name,
my heart throbs with tenderness.
My skin is pricked with needles of delight
and the tears flow unbarred.
I reach beyond my limbs.
Day and night, my love,
I think only of you.

My love has gone to a distant land
and here I am,
a hapless creature,
clinging to a wretched life.
My heart endlessly dotes
on recalling the feel of his touch.
And now some one else has enticed
that jewel away from me . . .

I shall compound a poison
and lay it on my tongue . . .

Should you encounter my disgraced face,
scandal will stain your world.
Go away home to your petty little ways,
you need never see these features again!

I shall abandon this wretched place
and take to the roads.
With a necklace of black gems about my throat,
I will wear earrings of Krishna's songs.
Arranged in a red robe of Krishna's devotion,
I shall be wandering from land to land
as a *yogini*[1] . . .

---

1. The female form of *yogi*, the ascetic, who has renounced the
   world for spiritual reasons.

. . . My life's precious jewel
fondles me with care
and I weigh the delight
on the scale of my heart.

As his desiring hands
surge with flooding strength,
my life climbs to nestle
straight into my hair . . .

I have never once heard
of such enchantment,
nor seen:
life clings to life
in a bondage of its own.

As parting weighs on the mind,
tears relieve the lovers
in each other's arms.
And each appears to die
in that half moment
when the face of love is screened
by an eyelid's drop . . .

Pouring perfumed water on Krishna's feet, Radha cleansed
and dried them with her own thick mass of hair. She then led
Krishna to the decorated bedstead and proceeded to anoint
Krishna's skin with cooling sandal paste blended with the scents of
musk and *aguru*. Radha continued to adorn Krishna with layer
upon layer of garlands of richly coloured flowers.

Once Radha's eyes registered Krishna's beauty, she could no
longer resist. She gazed and gazed upon Krishna's face. To Radha,
Krishna's face appeared as soothing and beautiful as the full moon.
Like the moon-bird *chakora*, Radha began to drink the nectar of
the moon.

Badu Chandidās

❖❖❖❖❖❖❖❖❖❖❖❖❖❖❖❖❖❖❖❖❖❖❖❖❖❖❖❖❖

The sun scalds me to death by day,
and the night moon crushes me with sorrow.
How can I suffer my life, dear friend[1],
sleep never visits my eyes.
I have moistened my skin
with cooling sandal paste,
and still I am seared by separation.

Break the earth open, O friend[2],
I would enter her womb
and hide . . .

---

1. & 2. Addressed by Radha to her friend Badāyi.

My youth and my wealth
are of no substance.
I shall tear away
my strings of pearls
and smash my armlets
to smithereens.
I shall wipe out
the red dust of love
from the parting of my hair
and shave my head clean.
I shall walk to the sea
on a pilgrimage.
As fate has robbed me
of my life-giving Kānha,
I shall dress as a *yogini*
and go to another land.
If my sacred deeds
do not join me with Kānha
in the act of making love,
I shall take poison
with my own hands . . .

With pain in her heart,
with tears in her eyes,
Radha[1] gazed at the road.
On a love-bed of flowers
as she waited brooding,
the moon lit the night
and a lamp illumined the room.
And all seemed so strange.
Why didn't Krishna come?
And all went in vain,
with half the night gone.

––––––––––

1. Daughter of Vrishabhānu

Swarming white ants of my memory
erode my love-spiced form
as I reflect upon my act of loving
black Krishna.

Day and night, in and out, at home
I fidget and twist.
Fear is my sole company
knowing black Krishna . . .

The trap is laid across the sky,
I have no way out . . .

What enchantment did I witness,
dear friend,
below the *kadamba* tree!
With life now wholly a wilderness,
I can no longer lead my heart to my home.
Bearing his beauty upon my eyes,
I shall deliver my life
to love's ever-growing forms . . .

ILLUSTRATIONS

1. Krishna's birthplace, Mathura, on the bank of the Jamuna.

2. Krishna as Vishnu's incarnation, portrayed with Vishnu's four arms and with the sect-marks of the Vishnu worshippers on his forehead and shoulders. On his sides, priests standing with a yaktail-plume and an offering bowl establish Krishna's divine origin. Udaipur (Rajasthan), late eighteenth century. Collection, Deben Bhattacharya.

3. A page from the illustrated manuscript of the *Gita Govinda* by Jayadeva describing the ten incarnations of Vishnu. Jodhpur (Rajasthan), c. 1750. Collection, Deben Bhattacharya.

4. A page from the illustrated manuscript of the *Gita Govinda* by Jayadeva describing the ten incarnations of Vishnu. Jodhpur (Rajasthan), c. 1750. Collection, Deben Bhattacharya.

5. *Vishnu in the body of a fish.* Illustration of Jayadeva's prayer to the ten incarations of Vishnu. Puri chitrapat (Orissa folk painting), c. 1955. Collection, Deben Bhattacharya.

6. *Vishnu in the body of a tortoise.* Illustration of Jayadeva's prayer to the ten incarnations of Vishnu. Puri chitrapa (Orissa folk painting), c. 1955. Collection, Deben Bhattacharya.

7. *Vishnu in the shape of a man-lion* (*Narasimha*). Illustration of Jayadeva's prayer to the ten incarnations of Vishnu. Puri chitrapat (Orissa folk painting), c. 1955. Collection, Deben Bhattacharya.

8. Krishna, with four arms, as Vishnu's incarnation. He is playing flute to the herd-girls and cows. Jodhpur (Rajasthan, c. 1775. Private collection, Jaipur. Photo: Ghanshyam Agrawal.

9. Krishna as a young cowherd in Gokul. Ajmer (Rajasthan), c. 1700. Private collection, Jaipur. Photo: Ghanshyam Agrawal.

10. *Bakāsuravadha.* Krishna killing the crane demon. Udaipur (Rajasthan), c. 1800. Private collection, Jaipur. Photo: Ghanshyam Agrawal.

11. *Bakasuravadha.* Krishna killing the crane demon. Puri chitrapat (Orissa folk painting), c. 1955. Collection, Deben Bhattacharya.

12. *Putanavadha.* Baby Krishna annihilating the ogress Putāna by sucking her breasts while his foster mother Yashodā runs after him. Puri chitrapat (Orissa folk painting), c. 1955. Collection, Deben Bhattacharya.

13. Krishna lifting Mount Govardhan to protect the cowherds from a torrential rain sent by Indra, the lord of the clouds. Udaipur (Rajasthan), c. 1750. Private collection, Jaipur. Photo: Ghanshyam Agrawal.

14. Krishna lifting Mount Govardhan. The trees on either side of Krishna symbolise his encouragement of the worshipping of the tree spirits by the cowherds in defiance of Indra, the lord of heaven. Ajmer (Rajasthan), c. 1700. Private collection, Jaipur. Photo: Ghanshyam Agrwal.

15. *Raga Meghamalhār.* Krishna dancing with herd-girls while playing a *Vinā* to the rainy-season-mode Raga Meghamalhār to invoke the clouds. Jodhpur (Rajasthan), c. 1700. Private collection, Jaipur. Photo: Ghanshyam Agrawal.

16. *Vastraharan.* Krishna teasing the herd-girls by stealing their clothes while they bathe in the Jamuna. Puri chitrapat (Orissa folk painting), c. 1955. Collection, Deben Bhattacharya.

17. *Face of Krishna.* While in the privacy of her terrace Radha makes up in front of a mirror, Krishna is already there, gazing at her. Bundi (Rajasthan), c. 1860. Private collection, Jaipur. Photo: Ghanshyam Agrawal.

18. *Rāslilā.* Herd-girls surround Krishna, all eager to dance with him. Bikaner (Rajasthan), c. 1800. Private collection, Jaipur. Photo: Ghanshyam Agrawal.

19. *Rasamandala.* Surrounded by the herd-girls on a night of the full moon, Krishna multiplies himself for the circular dance. Bundi (Rajasthan), c. 1750. Private collection, Jaipur. Photo: Ghanshyam Agrawal.

20. *Krishna in Spring.* A page from the illustrated manuscript of the *Gita Govinda* by Jayadeva giving the original text of *Raga Vasanta* (See page 32). Jodhpur (Rajasthan), c. 1750. Collection, Deben Bhattacharya.

21. *Krishna in Spring.* A page from the illustrated manuscript of the *Gita Govinda* by Jayadeva giving the original text of *Raga Vesanta* (See page 32). Jodhpur (Rajasthan), c. 1750. Collection, Deben Bhattacharya.

22. *Consolation to Radha.* A page from the illustrated manuscript of the *Gita Govinda* by Jayadeva representing the beginning of the ninth part. Jodhpur (Rajasthan), c. 1750. Collection, Deben Bhattacharya.

23. *Holi in Barsana.* The heralding drum of the Spring festival in Barsana, Radha's village in Braj.

24. *Holi in Barsana.* Young men from Nandgaon, Krishna's village, entering the street of Barsana with tortoise-shell shields (See page 15).

25. Spring festival at Radhavallabh temple in Brindaban.

26. Spring festival at Radhavallabh temple in Brindaban. Priests squirting water colours at the visitors during Holi.

27. *Krishna in Spring.* Krishna and the herd-girls squirting water colour during the Spring festival, Holi. Bikaner (Rajasthan), c. 1800. Private collection, Jaipur. Photo: Ghanshyam Agrawal.

28. *Krishna in Spring.* Krishna and the herd-girls squirting water colour during the Spring festival, Holi. Bundi (Rajasthan), c. 1750. Private collection, Jaipur. Photo: Ghanshyam Agrawal.

29. *Raga Vesanta.* Krishna dancing with Radha to the music of the Springtime mode, Raga Vasanta, as one herd-girl plays the rhythm on the frame drum and another squirts water colour at the dancers. Sirohi (Rajasthan), c. 1700. Private collection, Jaipur. Photo: Ghanshyam Agrawal.

नं केशवधृतलधरूपजय
निंदसियवविधरदरदक्षनिजां
सद्यरदयदर्शितयद्यघातं केश
वधृतबुधशरीरजयं॥४॥ म्लेछनि
वहनिधनेकलयसिकरगालं धूम
केतुमिवकिमयिकरगालं केशव
धृतकल्किशरीरजयं॥५॥ श्रीजय
देवकवेरिदंसुदितमुद्धारं श्रएफ
वदैस्कसदंसवसारं केशवधृतद
शविधरूपजयं॥७॥ वेदानुद्धरते
जगनिवहते भूगोलमुद्धिन्नते दैस्य
दारयतेवलिनिछलयतेदक्षसूयं

कुर्वतियौलस्यंजयतेहलंकलयनेक

एपतनेछब्लेज्ञातिंतौछ्या

रुमाचनेसूयदछछछ

यतुस्यंनमः॥श॥   ॥श॥   ॥श॥

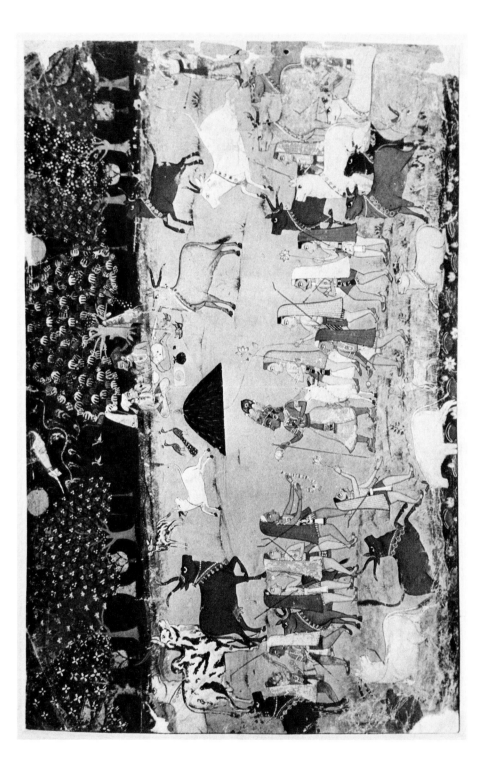

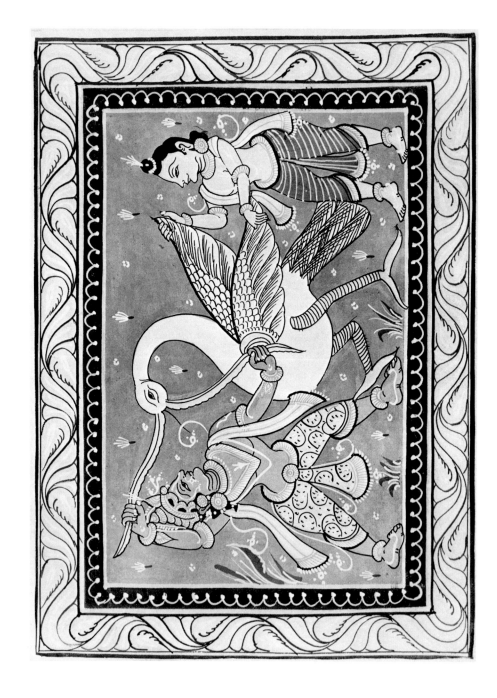

मेघमल्लाररागः

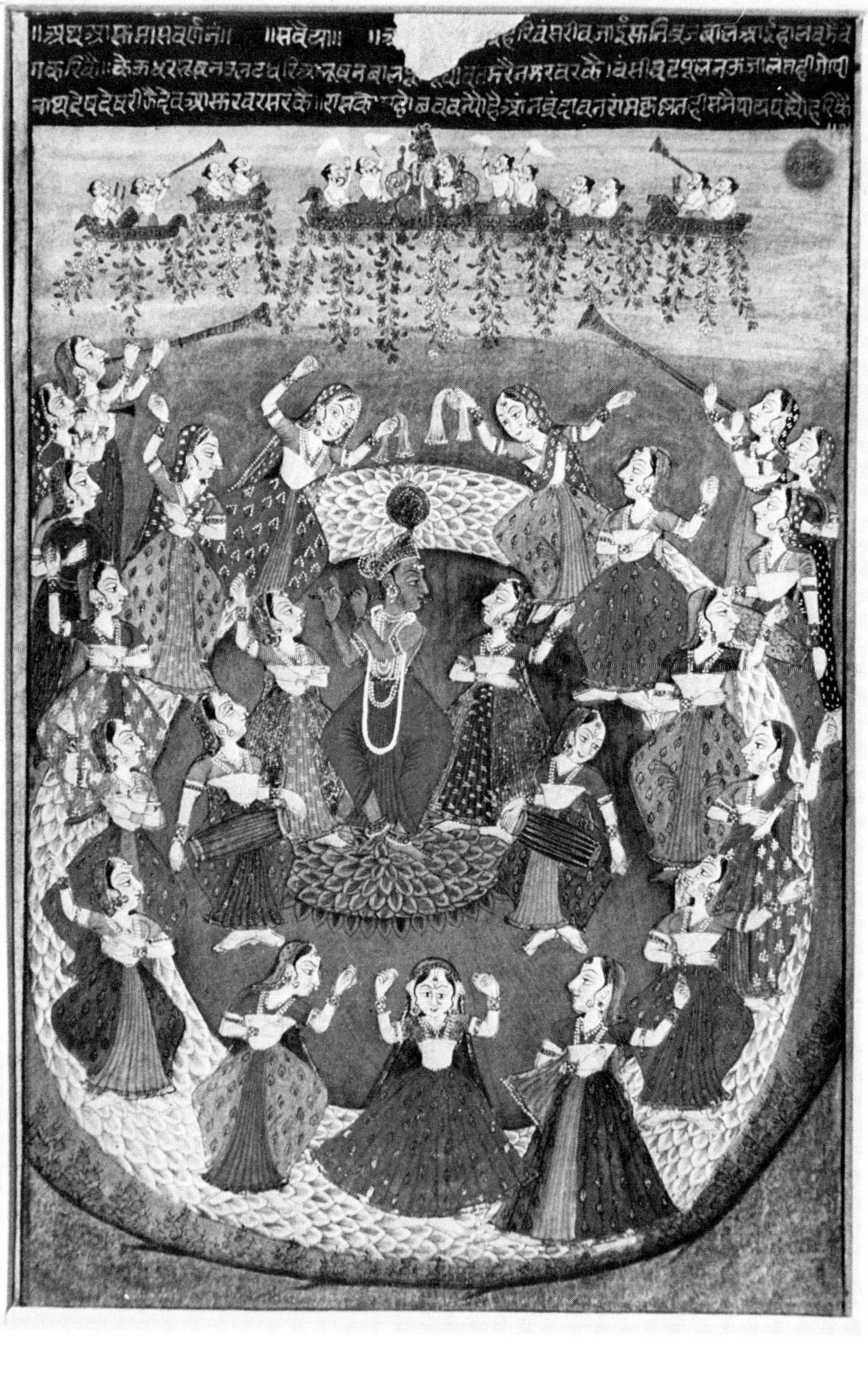
॥सवैया॥

काश्चे मिलितशिलीमुखपाटलप
रलकृतस्मरतूणविकाश्चे वि
हरति०विगलितलज्जितजाढवली
कलतरुणाकरुणाकृतड्रासे विरा
हिनिकृतनकुंतमुखादतिकेतकि
दंतुरिताश्चे पुप विहरति माधवि
काप्सिमललितनवमालतिजा
तिसुगंधौमुनिमनसामयिमोहन
काशिलितरुणाकारणबंधौ घाघा
विहरति०स्फुरदतिभुक्तलतापरि
रंभणासुकुलितपुलकितचूतै हं
दावनविपिनेपरिसरपरिगतया

मुनाजलयूति ॥९॥ विहरति०श्रीजय

सारं सरसवसंतसमयवनवर्ण

नमनुगतरतनविकारं ॥१०॥ विरं

क्षीयतिनामाष्टमःसर्गः॥८॥

अथतांमन्मथखिन्नांरतिरस
ज्ञिन्नांविषादसंपन्नां ऋतुवि
तितहरिचरितांकलहान्तरित
मुवाचरहःसखी ॥१॥

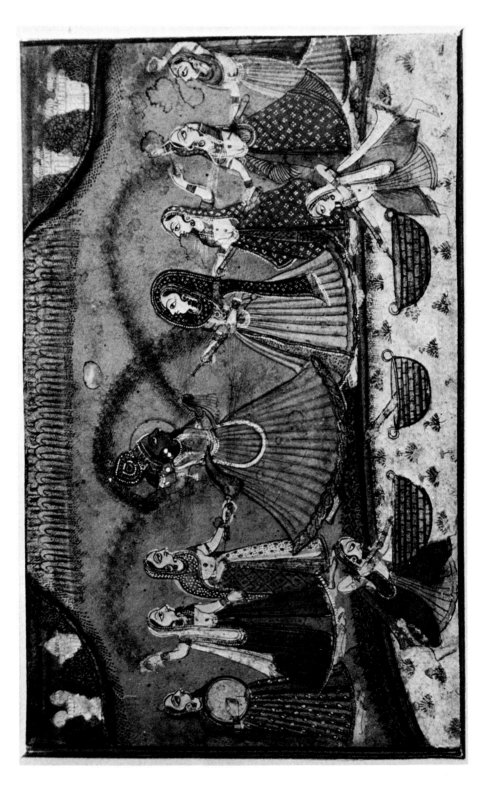

॥वसंतमदारागणी २१

Dwija Chandidās

❖❖

How should I live, dear friend,
and how much longer?
Krishna has struck me with a missile,
breaking a hole in my breast.
I shall now perish, my friend,
listening to the songs of his flute . . .

Tears obscure my path,
and my mouth is silent.
The necklace of enchantment,
the jewel of my care,
Krishna now plays his cruel flute
to murder my life . . .

I saw the dancer-moon
in the month of *Bhādar*[1]
when the rains came.
And from that very day
the myth of Kānu and me
sprang far and wide.

So many youthful girls
are living in Gokula
but the sounds of scandal
are scrawled on my fate alone.
My husband strikes with a stick
even on my shadows . . .

---

1. *Bhādar,* the month of rains during the period between the middle
   of August and the middle of September.

Who will then heed the heart,
the tales of my sadness,
if my beloved treats me as alien?
No one on this earth
may be called one's own.

Hoping for coolness
as I open my soul,
the fire redoubles.
And at last I know
that there is none in the worlds
of Gods, demons or men
who can be known as one's own.

I shall leave this land alone
for a far away place.

Govindadās

So long in the boundless sky the light of snow.
Unending scintillation of snow-rays—
    Lightning frozen in the clouds.

Elaborate, graceful, as the yak-tail plume
Flourished before the image of God,
    Loveliness enters the town.

So, Murderer, you raise your bow again.
Lost in your heart, Mādhav, I understand,
Sundered from one, you met many desires,
    Rāi was left alone.

You have held laughing even in the day the
People of moon-flowers, tinctured by a light
    Like a new colour of the sun.

Blossoming like the light of clustered pearls.
Gentle with power that gait of the elephant.
O peerless Lover, which of the city-girls
    Met you in love, I'll never know.

Everyone else knows, Govindadās retorts:
Kubjā, the hunchback, now is the new queen.[1]

---

1. Translated in collaboration with the late Lewis Thompson.

She casts her glances
as if unseeing,
and while I converse
she withholds her words.
Living encompassed
by lusty companions,
she laughs without laughing
at my jests.
As I behold
this beauty of Braj[1]
I fail to see—
is she woman or child?
The rays of her eyes
keep her secret.

And yet, she has forced
her way deep in my heart,
tearing open a breach
with love's flower-arrow.

---

1. The region of Braj, surrounding Mathura, Brindaban, Gokul and
   Govardhan in Northern India, is associated with Krishna's youth.

The scintillating rays of the moon
and the windblown granules of the rain
and a flower-strewn bed
with cushions of new leaves,
the soft southern breeze
and the soothing sandal paste,
combine to scorch him.

I believe that Krishna
is desirous of touching you.
Held in the passionate arms
of a beautiful girl,
he swoons, recalling you.

Like the new-laden clouds
that drape the surface of the earth,
his hair falls scattered
in a helpless mass.
Subtle is the remorse of love . . .

. . . Mādhava is avid
and the girl enchanted.
He is a connoisseur
of the flavours of love
and she wholly artless.
She repels his hands
when he reaches out
and her eyes well up only
as he gazes at her.
She trembles with fear
when he forces his way.
As he kisses her mouth
she covers her face
and takes to the earth
like a puppet in shock . . .

Why should you pluck flowers
in the forest,
my beautiful girl?
Your slender form is fashioned
by blossoms,
and your face
glows as a lotus of gold.
The black-bee, Krishna,
is drawn by its sweet smell . . .

I do know that you are bewitched
by the fragrance of my face,
fresh as a lotus bloom,
but I know not what is in your heart.
Cease that clamouring
so close to my spouse,
and stay away, Krishna,
O king of the black-bees.
Why do you hinder
my duties to my lord
and hum in my home
in your suffering thirst?
Go then, Krishna,
to the grove of love
where vines vibrate
with flowers aglow.

That was a signal
and Krishna set out . . .

The cloud is only a cloud of water
and lightnings singe the eyes.
Hard to touch are emerald and gold.
And yet this pair, fair skinned and dark,
have relighted my sight.
Their bodies and minds forever fresh,
Radha and Mādhava, matchless, shine.

What God has formed them
and brought them together
in a union of darkness and light?
Both, upheld in the flowing cups
of each other's eyes,
long for the lover's drink.
Their lips open for the nectar of desire
in a frenzy of loving—
and their bodies intermingle
in a tangle of arms,
searching—seeking the end.

When Radha retired
on the breast of Shyām,
suffering the lovers' fatigue,
her face resembled the graceful autumn night's moon.

As the image of love,
reclining, carved in emerald,
received her votive gift,
Radha sank like a garland of golden *champaka* bloom . . .

His face haloed
by the moon's matted hair,
traversing mountains, forests and pastures,
the lion casts scarlet frowns.
If you could arrest
in the cage of your heart
that restless lord,
you must be clever,
my beautiful girl
with the eyes of a doe.

So many loves
with glistening smiles
have tried to bar his hands—
but he bit their cheeks
and scarred their breasts
with ferocious claws—
strewing in the forest
their necklace pearls.
And so he lies
on a foliate bed,
waiting forever for you . . .

Breathing on his bamboo flute
he blew the pride of my clan away
like a fluff of cotton wool.
Faith in God and ethics
seem senile to me
and the name Woman aches in me
like the pain of revilement.
Friend, what is my way out?
Why do my very own limbs
now hinder my vision of Krishna?
Pinned by the arrow of flowers,
I blame my own eyes
for never glimpsing sleep.

While Krishna slept in the shrine of my heart
love kept vigil above us.
My pride of birthright had retreated
like a burglar on the run.
At last, O friend, my doubts dissolved.

Krishna's love, like a frog with the snake,
fell prey to my vanity of breeding.
Blind to my own true state,
I felt this and acted that,
though my heart was whole in love.

My husband to me was for swearing by,
to appease my captious kinsmen.

I could not hold the flow of my tears
and I wished that I knew
what had befallen my eyes.

Radha cries for Shyām
with Shyām in her arms:
"Where are you gone,
O lord of my life?"

Love knows no wisdom, O friend.
The lover embraces his love
and yet both, unaware, faint away
in anguish, estranged.

Shores of separation
are hidden from the eyes.

His beauty has filled
my whole vision
and as I remember
the sweet of his touch,
a sense of delight
never leaves my limbs.
My ears overladen
by the song of his flute,
listen to nothing else.
Friend, what use is your counsel now?

Love of Krishna
has made me impassioned—
body and mind
released from life's rules.
My nostrils are drunk
with the scent of his skin
and my tongue can take to
no other name.

Radha's comments

The sky is laden
with glamorous clouds.
Dark without.
I cannot see my own limbs,
but the face of Shyām,
shining like the moon in my heart,
rouses a tidal wave in me.
Friend, hold your questions—
the hour of the tryst is now!
Anoint me with black perfumes
of musk-deer in rut
and dress me in Krishna's blue.
Why should I bear
the bodice upon me?—
my breasts are full.
Throw away that string of pearls
which fetters me like a rival wife.
Now, my friend,
you peep through that hole
and see if the elders have fallen asleep.

Radha's friend protests

A solid door
closes the house from the world.
The path is slippery
and a frightening walk.
And the rains still rattle
rapidly down.
No blue wrap could
save you from the torrents,
my beautiful girl,
how can you keep the tryst?
Hari has his home
beyond the river of the mind.[1]
Thunder crashes
with deafening roars.
As my heart sinks in fear,
flashes of dazzling lightning
set space afire.
If you leave the house now,
O friend,
you will only die for love.

---

1. Mānas-gangā, lit. the Ganges of the [creator, Brahma's] mind.

Radha's response

I have crashed open the stout portals
of my family vows,
how can I be hindered by planks of wood?
I have already crossed the vast ocean
of my own self-esteem,
how deep can a river be for me?
Friend, do not try to test my strength.
Krishna scans my path
with uneasy mind
and my heart crumbles
brooding, brooding over it . . .

On a windblown December night
when the moon was encased
in the falling snow
and the world rested at home
shivering
draped to the eyes, huddled for warmth,
Radha set out for the tryst.
I was startled to see, O friend,
that she left the comfort of bed—
and wrapped her body in a white cloth.
Her breasts, thrusting forth in her bodice,
seemed inflamed
as she walked to the grove, unseen.
Her delicate feet that could not dent the snow flakes,
were torn by thorns,
and yet,
she did not flinch.

The sun stood high overhead
and the sand burned on the streets.
The glare radiated heat.
And yet, she set out for the tryst
in broad daylight.
Her form was as tender as a statue of cream,
and her feet fell like lotus blooms.

God, how irresistible are the steps of love.
Guided by the delight of Krishna's caresses,
she had lost her reason.
The eyes of her elders barricaded her way
and the wind uplifted a blind of dust,
but the playmate of love had cast all aside
to take to the path of the tryst.

. . . Arrows were discharged
from the eyes to the eyes
and the arms were engaged
in reconnaissance.
Then the bodies engaged at close quarters.
The conquest was complete.

How did you leave your home today?
I wished to know the nature of your love!
Did you not tremble in fear of your elders?
Dense darkness had curtained all eyes.
How could you see your path at night?
My heart had kindled the lamp of love.
How could you walk this distant way?
I rode on the chariot of my mind.
How could you travel alone so far?
The knight of the flower-arrow marched in front.

And then as each reached the other,
their bodies met in a single form.

Mādhava, how can I describe her anguish?
You are roused in her heart as you leave her rooms deserted;
that graceful girl, in the grief of parting,
desolately paints a portrait of you.

But the cruel God hindered her again:
While drawing one thing she outlined another.
As she limned your face, the moon came in sight
and in her confusion, she gazed and gazed.
Your brows transformed into the bows of Love
and your eyes resembled his arrows of bloom.
She swooned as she saw your form transmuting
into the body of the bodiless God.

How else could she design your expression?
She stayed transfixed like a statue on the wall.

I have not seen
his graceful moonlit face,
now the moon beams burn my eyes.

I have not heard
his sweet charmed voice, now the bees' songs rasp in my ears.

Friend, why did I fan my pride?
Sundered from his love,
in fear I now ache.
Will you then appear to my Krishna for me?

I have ignored
his soft foliate hands,
now the leaves nettle my skin.

I have discarded
the garland threaded by him,
my necklace has changed to a snake.

I have forsaken
the nectar of new life,
now my body is a storehouse of poison.

Has Krishna then gone to the city of Mathura?
Gokula is made empty today.
The parrots cry out in their cages
and the cattle race for Mathura.
The banks of the Jamuna are still as they were
but silent of the cowherds' calls.
I shall abandon myself in the sea
and be born as Kāna in another life.
Krishna will then be born as Radha
and learn to feel the pain of parting.

Mirābāi

The flute still sings on the Jamuna bank.

I hear the flute
and I cannot endure.
My heart dissolves in Krishna.

Black Krishna.
Black lotus.
Black river.

I hear the cadence
of Krishna draw near
and I climb to the tower
to look out.
Friend, when will my lord be here?

As peacocks, frogs and the rain-birds[1] call
and the kokilas are clothed in loveliness,
Indra, the rain-god, roars in the sky
joining all.
While lightning abandons shame,
the earth glows with ever-new forms.

---

1. *Papaiyā*

Clouds of the month of *shrāvana,*[1]
The longing of *shrāvana:*
Shrāvana enchants my heart
With the sounds of Krishna's steps.
Lightnings flash. As the storms rage,
Layer upon layer of gathering clouds
Burst in gentle showers . . .

---

1. *Shravāna:* The monsoon month between the middle of July and
   the middle of August.

The alleys are closed for me,
how can I walk to join Krishna?
The road is rugged and slick
and my unsteady feet
falter again and again
as I figure my pace
with judgement and care.
I can hardly climb the stages
to the palace of my love—
long, long away.
My heart proceeds by jolts.

Mile after mile the road is guarded
as brigands watch.
O God, what made you plant my village
so terribly afar?

I must absolutely see you,
my sweet love.

I think of you,
I reflect upon you
and I contemplate you.

I go dancing
on the dust of your feet
wherever your steps
descend on this earth.

Songs in praise of God
are my imperishable trust.

I observe no other forms of prayer
or pilgrimage or meditation—
they only leave me void.
Sacred chants and diagrams
and visits to Varanasi
to study the Vedic scriptures
say nothing to me.

Krishna alone is the lord of Mirā,
and she, at his lotuslike feet, serves.

Shyām has become as invisible
as the new crescent moon
of the second lunar night.
And that dweller of Madhuban
had thrown a lasso of love at me
when I was there.

Now the fervour seems to have waned.

Who babbles
of my lord's enchanting return?
He never came to visit me
nor wrote a line;
I suffered deep, my trust is lost.

My eyes, defying my words,
flow like a river at monsoon flood.
What may I do—?
for nothing is in my control.
I have no wings
or else I should simply fly to him.

Song-bird, *papaiyā*,
do not twitter of my sweet love.
Sundered from him, when I hear you
I feel like wringing your wings
and clipping your beaks
and adding black coloured[1] salt to the wound.

My sweet love is mine
and I am his own—
why should you call him darling?
If only I could join my lover today,
your songs would sound so sweet.
I would gild your beaks in layers of gold
and covet you as the crown to my head . . .

---

1. Colour of Krishna.

If I had known
that falling in love
was to fall in with pain,
I would have thundered a drum
to proclaim through the city
that love was banned for all . . .

Not seeing you,
my eyes sting.
Since you left
I have no rest.
When I hear a sound
my heart trembles—
but that in itself
is sweet, lovely . . .

Sleep does not visit me
the whole night long—
how can the day dawn?
Startled, when I rise
from my reverie,
I see the insomniac moon . . .

When the whole world
rests in slumber, dear love,
I keep vigil, riven from him.
In a glorious palace of pleasure,
estranged, I sit awake,
and see a forsaken girl,
with a garland of tears on her neck,
passing the night
counting stars,
counting the hours
to happiness.

Anantadās

I ceaselessly scanned for Kānu
that thick dark night
and I knew how hard men were.
As clouds roared and rolled,
frogs, in love, intoned the season's song
and crickets strummed their strings.
My heart rocked like a doll
when lightning crashed the dark . . .

The master of love
came with masses of blossoms
and arrayed them upon me.
He took the comb in his hand
and dressed my hair,
mounting plait upon plait.
My joy, O friend, was speechless!
A clove-scented vine
scorched in a forest fire,
I was about to flower once more.
Like the lotus in the season of snow,
living, I was dead,
but the rays of the striking sun
made me bloom again.

Unhindered by separation
I have plumbed the sea of undying delight.
How can I then describe my mind
in its boundless turmoil?
I have thrown my calm and shame away
to fulfill his heart's desire.

He gave me my life
and I am his expression now.

As their bodies relaxed
after the circular dance,
both took their seats
on the waves of joy . . .

Narottamdās

This night of rain and rapture, all
Brindāban, unmoored, adrift—
Lost in the solid dark of rain,
        In torrents of sweet rain.

Wild lightning in the lap of darkness,
Radha ever more richly plays.
While sidelong in the slippery path
A way is felt, vermilion, musk
And sandal-mark all turn to mud,
        In torrents of sweet rain.

Narottama, who cannot swim,
Drowns in the unhorizoned sea.[1]

---

1. Translated in collaboration with the late Lewis Thompson.

Jadunandandās

When Radha sinks in a faint
and her breathing no longer flows
and all her friends, as one,
repeat your name in her ears,
her senses return . . .

When Kānu proceeded to the pastoral field,
Rāi restlessly suffered, sundered from him.
In anguish of parting, she entreated her friends:
"How could I join the son of Nanda?—
The forest is thick with herds of cows
and crowded with herdsmen from the clan.
How could I reach him in this day's broad light?"

Jnānadās

❖❖❖❖❖❖❖❖❖❖❖❖❖❖❖❖❖❖❖❖❖❖❖❖❖❖

Given over, both, to the combat of delight—
Unflagging lightning in new clouds of rain:
Radha and Kāna on a couch of flowers.
Both hearts inveigled by the mind-born god,
Again and again they kiss with startled eyes,
Her little breasts ravished by violent nails.
To see them at their love-sport in the bower,
What joy reigns in the heart of Jñānadās.[1]

---

1. Translated in collaboration with the late Lewis Thompson.

My eyes flow for his lovely form
and my heart is filled with his excellence.
Each part of my being
cries for each part of his,
and my heart for his heart's meeting.
My life longing for love
cannot rest still.
I must carry out my vow, dear friend.

How can I describe that rise of joy
only—only to see him?
My body agitates for his physical touch.
The essence of my love with his gentle smiles
releases a stream of sweetness for me.
I live with friends, amidst proud elders,
and as I hear them talk of Shyām,
needles of delight prickle my skin.
I try to cover the signs of my love
and my eyes flow unbarred.

The vision of beauty rests
by the black-river[1] bank—
unmatched enchantment
in the *kadamba* shade.
Lightning is frozen
in the cloudscape
as peacocks make dance.
And the moon still shines
in a circle of black-bees.
The shadow antelope is gone . . .

---

1. Kalindi = Jamuna

. . . My eyes remain drowned
in the ocean of beauty.
I have lost my heart
in the forest of young love . . .

In the fragrant new Spring of flowers
the moon irradiated the night
and the southern breeze
carried the sandalwood scent.
The *kokilas* sang
and the black-bees sported with love.

In a night such as this
Radha with her followers dressed
for a walk to the river bank.
The air was cool
when Radha met Krishna
and his circle of friends.
Each engaged the other,
their gazes locking,
and with smiles on their lips.

When their throats drew nearer
and the faces met
and the hearts became one,
passion spread.
With love in their hearts
as they reclined on the bed,
shyness intervened
and they could not reveal themselves.

The room was lit
by a bejewelled lamp
and their bodies glistened
on a flower-strewn bed . . .

Their eyes spoke
the language of love.
Only the lovers
shared the sense
of their hearts—
the others sensed nothing.
Friend, such artful lovers
are Radha and Krishna.

Krishna crossed his arms
and hugged his chest—
Radha knew her lover
craved embraces.
She touched her hair—
the signal of the darkening night.

Krishna closed his face
in his open hands—
a lotus asleep within a lotus bloom.
The night was now.
She was eager
says Jñānadās:
the tryst was agreed.

Friend, O friend,
look what my body does to me.
Love of Shyām
is the life of my life
and yet, I cannot see
where I should go with my being.
God has lashed me down
without strings.

Krishna flatters me
as if he were my slave,
his voice reaching out like a dream.
The more he shows his passion,
the greater my regrets.
I avoid his contact
as of boiling oil.
As anger rises within me,
my heart sports on the swing of love.

He has burgled my heart
by his glances alone
and has robbed me of vision
by his spellbinding form.
Life itself is my witness:
my feelings are afloat
on the waves of the enchanted age.

Krishna has made me an outcast
to the ways of the world.
My heart is filled wholly
with the flashings of his eyes,
his smiles and his speeches
and the postures of his head.
The breeze that brushes the skin of Krishna
turns life into gold.

I long to proceed
but my feet neither
go nor stand still.
No more do I nurse
any hope or despair—
my heart breeds
a harvest of fear . . .

While Krishna stayed away,
the rains came
and the lightning flashed
in the reaches of space.
How shall I deceive the hours of the day—?
my life is at stake.
That pitiless lord is still not here.

My heart in an uproar rebounds
to the thunderous roars of the clouds.
And at night as I gaze out,
my life departs
with the windblown showers from the sky . . .

Watching your path
she has blinded her eyes.
She has blunted her fingertips
counting the days.
Days upon days
have mounted to months
and the months into a year.
Now it is year after year.

Mādhav, what kind of a promise
is this? . . .

Merciless Krishna, you may hear now that Radha is pining away. When she reaches to the lotus-bloom bed, a shock forces her life out. And as she detects the moon in the autumn night, she is ready to relinquish her being. She sheds her tears in the company of friends, recalling the past play of love. When she broods bending her head, her entire body is frozen still. And then the heat begins to rise in her limbs—in wave upon wave of liquid fire. Her body trembles with such awesome force that none can restrain her. And a long-held sigh escapes her.

Rādhāmohandās

The contact brought
a murmur of joy
amid words of denials
and needles of delight
on enraptured limbs . . .

A mouth smiled
and a mouth drank
the breathing sighs.
Eyes stood still
over lowered eyelids . . .

Vanished the heat of the ignited noon
when Radha and Mādhav joined each other
in a temple on an island in a lake.
Rippling water sprayed crystals of coolness
and the soft breeze carried the scent of flowers.
How could the sun's rays hinder them?

The enchantress[1]
and the master enchanter
are joyously engrossed in the dance of delight.
Their rhythmed ringing voices
sing the many chords of love.
The moon mounts the sky
and the light returns.

---

1. Binodini (Radha).

Ragas and rhythms
are housed in your bosom—
you have mastered
the mysteries of music,
its octaves and its scales.

Teach me then the secrets of the sweet prelude[1]
I shall banish my bamboo flute
and, sitting near you,
learn your enchanting songs.
Proceed with my lessons,
mouth upon mouth, and
I shall spread broad my breast.

1. *Ālāp,* the improvised prelude which prefaces a Rāga.

He guessed—and acted.
Joyously jingled the ankle-bells
and bracelets thundered the hour of war;
deep embraces and twining arms
locked their bodies in brave combat.
The time was ripe
for love's encounter
and its age-long kisses
in a rhythm of gold . . .

Ballabhadās

❖❖❖❖❖❖❖❖❖❖❖❖❖❖❖❖❖❖❖❖❖❖❖❖❖❖❖❖❖❖

Each tenderly left the other's body
and rose to rest on a bed strewn with flowers.
Friends smiled at that unwonted act
but as body quit body
the bodiless God of love
came into view . . .

Uddhabadās

❖❖❖❖❖❖❖❖❖❖❖❖❖❖❖❖❖❖❖❖❖❖❖❖❖❖❖❖❖❖❖❖

Radha was the body of love
and Shyām the great connoisseur.

Glimpsing her own reflection
in the mirror of Shyām's limbs,
Radha mistaken, in anger turned away.
"How can he be so cruel—
to play with another
before my very eyes?"
Ignoring Kāna
she left with protesting pride.

Friends begged and implored her
and Uddhabadās prayed.

The season of frost,
the chilling wind,
the rays of the moon—
she shivers all the more,
in the fever of separation.
How much, O God, can a frail girl endure
with this anguish of parting?
The night lingers without end
as she longs sleepless for the dawn.
Then joyously turning to the eastern sky
she breaks and howls.

Hear my words on the game of enchantment:
Toying together in the festival of Spring,
the lovers have transfigured each into other.
Blind with the red dust[1] of the season's rites,
wiping their eyes they kiss
and the syringe ejects torrents of crimson dawn.
Who can tell
who is the man
and who the woman
in this ecstasy?

_____

1. During the *holi*, the annual Spring festival; the colour red
   symbolises love. See Introduction p. 15, and illustrations Nos.
   26-28.

Kabishekhar

Walking in the lanes:
as Radha and Kāna's eyes joined,
both hearts became the targets
of the mind-born God—
and each fell possessed by the other's face.
The dumb robber had no sense of time,
but the beloved girl, wise in love,
warned him with a glance.
Each took to the main street,
hiding a heart.

~~~~~~

The days of laughing glances
and beckoning smiles are gone, sweet love.
How you used to clear the forests
of all the flowers in the land for me.
Now in love with the charms of the town,
you cannot even recall my face . . .

Balarāmdās

❖❖❖❖❖❖❖❖❖❖❖❖❖❖❖❖❖❖❖❖❖❖❖❖❖❖❖❖❖❖❖❖

Each encountered the other
—their eyes conjoining
with sight blotted out in a clash of delight.
Their joyous babbling lulled into silence,
they stood numb with fierce passion.
Sighting their target across a damaged bow,
they struck the mark with arrows of love . . .

~~~~~~~~~~~~~~~~~~~~~~~~~~~~~~~~

The pollen, sprayed
from the open flowers,
float on the air
of all the forest—
spreading perfume.
Drunk with honey
the swarming bees,
adrift, enter
the grove of love—
singing aloud.
Kokilas chant
the sweet thunder,
the cry of delight,
for the heart's lord—
driving him wild.
As the moon ascends
the glowing night,
the row of trees
with tender leaves
stands glittering . . .

Shame on your affections, Shyām,
and disgrace to the girl who adores you.
You are sham, sly and swift—
what use then are your bewitching speeches?
Spontaneous fire consumes my limbs—
why do you feed it with the language of guile?
The beauty you desire is a woman of merit,
and artless am I in the parleys of pleasure.
Let her then fulfill the wish of your heart
for whom you deceive me the whole night long . . .

~~~~~~

They are raising scandals about him—
I do not see him with my open eyes.
Of all those girls
that inhabit the city,
who does not turn to gaze at Shyām? . . .
But with me all whirls
upside down—
they spread my secrets throughout the world . . .

. . . The more he made love to me
the more was written on my heart,
word after word.
With a smile he delivered a message
that cut open my ribs.
When I recall it now,
my heart seethes like a mine afire . . .

Like the evil shadow[1]
that screens the moon,
her dishevelled hair
enshrouded her lovely face.
Kisses swept away
those scarlet signs
and the lamp-black
that had lined her glistening eyes
vanished with the vermilion dust of love.

Krishna, you have a ruthless heart
to treat my friend in such a fashion.
Her lips are slashed by your biting teeth
and her necklace torn
in your raider's bed.
Her flowering breasts
have suffered your harrowing nails
as you crushed the body
that housed the bodiless God . . .

1. Rāhu, the evil force that is said to cause the lunar eclipse.

Bedecked with blossoms
as the new foliage swayed,
the bees hummed
and the honey-queen drank.
The new-born *kokilas*
sang the fifth note
and the lovers were caressed
by the sandalwood wind . . .

Each seeing each,
each was possessed—
each becoming the other.

~~~~~~~~~~~~~~~~~~~~~~~~~~~~~~~~~~~~

Who in my reach
will visit the city of Mathura
and carry the note from my anguished heart?
I have written recalling his moon-graced face—
my hand become a pen,
my eyes inkwells,
and my heart charred as kohl
for the writing ink . . .

NOTES ON THE POETS

The names of the poets are listed chronologically following the order of their appearance in the book.

JAYADEVA, late twelfth century. Father: Bhojadeva. Mother: Bamadevi. Born in Kendubilva, West Bengal. Patron: King of Orissa. Author of the *Gita Govinda* (Songs of the Cowherd), written in Sanskrit.

VIDYĀPATI, born 1352 (see Subhadra Jha in the *Songs of Vidyāpati*, Banaras, 1954) and died 1448. Born at Bisapi, Madhubani, north-east Bihar. Author of *Kirtilatā* (Vine of Glory), written between 1370-80 under the patronage and in praise of Kirti Simha, the King of Mithila; Bhuparikramā (Round the World); Likhanāvali (On Writing Sanskrit); and several other works including five hundred famous songs on Radha and Krishna's love. Patrons: the kings of Mithila, including Siva Simha who ruled between 1402 and 1406. Wrote in Sanskrit and (the love songs of Krishna) in Maithili.

CHANDIDĀS, late fourteenth century. Lived in Chhatna (District Bankura) and in Nannur (District Birbhum) in West Bengal. Occupation: temple priest. Chandidās is considered the most important Vaishnava poet in Bengal. Several other poets, during various periods, have adopted his name, such as, BADU CHANDIDĀS and DWIJA CHANDIDĀS. Wrote in Bengali.

GOVINDADĀS, born 1381 and died 1457. Father: Chiranjib Sen. Mother: Sunanda. Born in Shrikhanda (District Burdwan), West Bengal. Wrote in Bengali and Brajbuli, an artificial language compounded from Bengali and the dialect of Braj.

MIRĀBĀI, born c. 1500 and died 1546. Father: Ratna Simha Kurki, belonging to the princely family of Merhta. Born in Kurki, about 35 kilometers from Merhta city in Rajasthan. Wrote in Rajasthani, Gujrati and in Hindi.

ANANTADĀS, born c. fifteenth century. A disciple of Shri Chaitanya (1486-1533). Wrote in Bengali.

NAROTTAMDĀS, born c. middle of fifteenth century. Father: Krishnananda Datta. Mother: Narayani Dasi. Born in the village Kheturi (District Rajsahi) in Bengal. Author of *Prembhaktichandrikā* and *Prembhaktichintāmani*. Wrote in Bengali.

JADUNANDANDĀS, c. sixteenth century. Lived in Malihati, Bengal. Author of *Karnānanda Kāvya* and several translations from Sanskrit. Wrote in Bengali and Brajbuli.

JNĀNADĀS, c. sixteenth century. Born in the village Kandra (District Birbhum) in West Bengal. Wrote in Bengali and Brajbuli.

RĀDHĀMOHANDĀS, born 1688 and died 1778. Renowned scholar, poet and musicologist. Compiler of an important anthology of Vaishnava songs, entitled *Padāmritasamudra*. Wrote in Bengali and Brajbuli.

BALLABHADĀS, c. seventeenth century. Wrote in Bengali and Brajbuli.

UDDHABADĀS, born second half of the eighteenth century in the village of Tainya Baidyapur, Bengal. He was a disciple of the poet Rādhāmohandās. Wrote in Bengali and Brajbuli.

KABISHEKHAR, c. eighteenth century, at Parangram (District Burdwan), West Bengal. Wrote after the style of the poet Govindadās in Bengali and Brajbuli. Author of *Gopālavijaya kāvya*, which consisted of two thousand couplets and was completed in 1779.

BALARĀMDĀS, date unknown. Born at Shrikhanda (District Burdwan), West Bengal. Father: Ātmārām Dās. Mother: Soudāmini. Wrote in Bengali and Brajbuli.

Bibliography

Bengali

Bandyopadhyay, Saroj, (ed.) *Vaishnava Padaratnāvali,* Calcutta, 1961.

Basumati Sahitya Mandir, (Publishers), *Vaishnava Mahājan Padavali,* Calcutta, no date.

Basu, Shankariprasad, *Chandidās O Vidyāpati,* Calcutta, 1960.

Bhattacharya, Byomakesh, *Mirabai,* Varanasi, 1957.

Lahiri, Durgadas, *Vaishnava Padalahari,* Calcutta, 1905.

Mazumdar, Bimanbihari, *Chandidāser Padāvali,* Calcutta, 1960 *Pānchshata Batsarer Padavali,* Calcutta, 1961 and *Shodash Shatābdir—Padāvali-Sāhitya,* Calcutta, 1961.

Mitra, Khagendra Nath and others, (eds.) *Vaishnava Padāvali,* (fifth edition), Calcutta University, Calcutta, 1956.

Mukhopadhyay, Harekrishna, *Vaishnava Padāvali,* Calcutta, 1961.

Ray, Kalidas, *Padāvali Sāhitya,* Calcutta, 1961, and *Prāchin Banga* Calcutta, no date.

Sahana, Satyakinkar, *Chandidās-Prasanga,* Calcutta, 1959.

Sen, Sukumar, (ed.) *Vaishnava Padāvali,* New Delhi, 1957.

Hindi

Benipuri, Rambriksha, (ed.) *Vidyāpati ki Padāvali,* (fourth edition), Patna, 1996 (Vikram year).

English

Archer, W.G., *The Loves of Krishna,* London, 1957; New York, 1960.

Aurobindo, Sri, (transl.) *Songs of Vidyāpati,* Pondicherry, 1956.

Basham, A.L., *The Wonder that was India,* London, 1954.

Bhattacharya, Deben, (transl.) *Love Songs of Vidyāpati,* ed. W.G. Archer, London, 1963, Delhi, 1967; New York 1970. *Love Songs of Chandidās,* London 1967; New York, 1970.

Keyt, G., (transl.) *Sri Jayadeva's Gita Govinda,* Bombay, 1947.

Roy, P.C., (transl.) *The Mahabharata,* Calcutta, 1883.

Varma, Monika, (transl.) *The Gita Govinda of Jayadeva,* Calcutta, 1968.

Discography

BAM LD 5014 *Ragas de Benares,* Editions disc AZ, Paris.

BAM LD 5099 *Religious Songs from Bengal,* Edition disc Az, Paris.

ZFB 52 *Songs of Krishna,* Argo (Decca), London.

FE 4431 *Religious Music of India,* Folkways, New York.